# A PRACTICAL GUIDE TO
# ORGANIZATIONAL ENGINEERING

J.R. Paul Lanthier

A PRACTICAL GUIDE TO

# ORGANIZATIONAL ENGINEERING

J.R. Paul Lanthier

ISBN 978-1-941872-62-8
HF062023

© 2014-2023 Reliabilityweb, Inc.
Printed in the United States of America.
All rights reserved.

This book, or any parts thereof, may not be reproduced, stored in a retrieval system, or transmitted in any form without the permission of the Publisher.
Opinions expressed in this book are solely the author's and do not necessarily reflect the views of the Publisher.

Publisher: Reliabilityweb, Inc.
Cover Design: Jocelyn Brown
Layout and Design: Chip McGoldrick

For information: Reliabilityweb.com
www.reliabilityweb.com
8991 Daniels Center Drive, Suite 105, Ft. Myers, FL 33912
Toll Free: 888-575-1245 | Phone: 239-333-2500
E-mail: crm@reliabilityweb.com

10  9  8  7  6  5

# Table of Contents

## Preface ..................................................................................... III

## Asset Management Business Process ......... 1

Why Define a Business Process? ....................................................... 1

Current Asset Management Business Processes ......................... 2

World-Class Asset Management Business Process Elements ..... 4

Steps in Defining and Mapping the Business Process Elements .. 6

Quality Measures ................................................................................. 9

A Better Approach to RACI ................................................................. 9

Macro and Micro Deployment Strategies ....................................... 10

## Effective Staffing and Training ........................... 13

The Role of Human Resources ........................................................ 13

Defining Skills and Abilities at the Task Level ................................ 14

Task-Specific Training and Coaching ............................................. 14

Developing a Training Program ....................................................... 15

Improving the Training Program ...................................................... 16

Effective Staffing ................................................................................ 16

## Efficient Meetings ........................................................... 19
Why do Meetings Fail? ........................................................ 19
Structuring Your Meetings .................................................. 20
The Four Types of Meetings ............................................... 23
Meeting Maps ..................................................................... 24
Auditing Meetings to Ensure Effectiveness and Efficiency ......... 26

## Effective Key Performance Indicators ...... 29
KPIs as Value Focusing Tools ............................................. 29
Normalizing Our Definitions ............................................... 30
KPI Categories .................................................................. 31
Assuring Results ............................................................... 32
Applying KPIs to Performance Management Plans ................ 34
Rules for Defining KPIs ..................................................... 34
KPI Parameter Definition Template .................................... 42
KPI Hierarchy .................................................................... 43
Physical Asset Management KPI Examples ....................... 46

## Deployment ........................................................................ 51
Deployment versus Implementation ................................... 51
Communication Plan .......................................................... 52
Transition Plan/Maturity Plan ............................................. 54
Control Plan ....................................................................... 54

## Conclusion ........................................................................ 57

## Bio .................................................................................... 58

# Preface

The world of maintenance has made substantial advances in the past 50-70 years. From a repair when needed approach, maintenance has evolved with the introduction of planning and scheduling, software tools, preventive and predictive maintenance concepts, practices and technologies and reliability and asset management philosophies. Yet, throughout all of these evolutions the one truism cannot be ignored: organizations are made up of people. The efficient and effective use of our human resources is essential to achieving maximum, sustainable benefits from our improvement programs and organizational strategies.

A Dofasco (ArcelorMittal) commercial used to say: "Our product is steel. Our strength is people." This is very true. Sustainable growth and success relies heavily on the quality and roles of the people that make up our organization. Unfortunately, due to economic pressures and skill shortages, our teams are shrinking and many organizations are becoming increasingly people dependent instead of system dependent. As a result, we too often adapt our business process to the skills currently available in the organization, rather than adapting the people to the process.

I recently read an alarming statistic that *90 percent of improvement initiatives fail.* I also read that 85 percent of reliability centered maintenance (RCM) analyses are not implemented (reliabilityweb.com). Statistics like these confirm that a significant portion of our efforts to improve do not deliver the anticipated and much needed results. Why?

Improvement initiatives fail due to:

- A lack of vision (agreed upon and effectively communicated);
- Little or no active sponsorship from management;
- An underestimation of the effort to develop and deploy the initiative;
- An absence of plans to deal with the unexpected.

Even if improvement initiatives are in place and they are successful, an organization must also look at the long term and determine how to sustain – and continue to develop – initiatives in perpetuity. An obvious answer is continued effort and commitment. But a better answer is to develop an organization that logically provides the end results we are expecting. As W. Edwards Deming once said: "Your systems are perfectly designed for the results you are getting." Sustaining successful initiatives requires improving our systems. That is, we must define the best in class business processes that support our vision of the future, sustain these processes with qualified resources, manage them through efficient meetings, and control them through effective Key Performance Indicators (KPIs).

Commodity price variations, a widening talent gap, resource shortages, increased costs associated with wages, taxes and capital investments, and a need to do more with less through staff reductions are making it more difficult to sustain our objectives. Yet the need to sustain our objectives is even more imperative if we want to survive. Tightening our belts or running faster are not answers – we have been doing so for years with little to show for it. The solution is a fundamental shift in how we do business. This includes how we hire and train our resources, our ability to define and run effective meetings and our ability to identify and utilize KPIs that support our business model and drive us towards operational excellence.

This book is a practical guide to developing and deploying a world-class physical asset management organization. We will review the concepts of roles and responsibility mapping to define a best in class organization, as well as a simpler, better way to define and apply a responsible, accountable, consulted, informed (RACI) model. We will also discuss how to develop the necessary skills within your team. Once the business process is deployed, we manage it through meetings and control it through KPIs. We will discuss how to develop meaningful meetings and KPIs, in support of the business process, and how to use these to engineer an efficient and effective organization that is sustainable and evolves with your needs and level of maturity.

# Asset Management Business Process

## Why Define a Business Process?

*"Defining a business process takes time, which we do not have. It is an activity that does not solve the immediate issues we are facing, such as producing more despite the constraints. It is fundamentally a good idea, as a future project, but if we do not start producing more right now there will be no future."*

This is a typical answer to the prospect of defining an asset management business process and – based on the results usually achieved by this exercise – it makes perfect sense, though it is not the right answer. W. Edwards Deming said, "You must know what to do and then do your best." A well defined and **applied** business process that supports a long-term strategy increases workforce efficiency and provides the means to meet today's requirements while setting the stage to meet tomorrow's. Without it, we will remain reactive at the organizational level.

Years ago, I worked with a mine to help them develop the organization and programs necessary to become proactive, using reliability principles. This included defining and applying a best in class asset management business process. When asked what this had done for him, the superintendent of the mobile fleet answered: "Up to one and a half years ago I used to be called at home every night [to resolve some problem]. Now I never get phone calls." In other words, we are now in control.

To be in control we need to follow a process. However, steps in defining this process must be reasonable and practical, and the results easily applied. The exercise must also provide measurable, sustainable results. In this chapter we will:

- Look at current asset management business processes;

- Identify the elements that make up a world-class asset management process;

- Describe and map the steps in defining the process elements;

- Define the quality measures to incorporate in order to successfully apply and control the process;

- Look at a better way to do RACI roles assignments;

- Describe how to deploy the new roles and responsibilities – the macro versus micro approach.

# Current Asset Management Business Processes

I tend to separate these based on the various framework origins, which can be summed up as: quality, operations and maintenance.

Quality initiatives and thought processes have given birth to Sustainable Development, Six-Sigma and the Dofasco process:

- Sustainable Development takes the approach that we will improve by measuring, communicating the results, and taking action to resolve. It includes a series of audits as well as KPIs.

- Six-Sigma is all about failure elimination by focusing on relevant issues and resolving them. It involves measuring and identifying failures in order to put together solutions.

- The Dofasco process originated from Total Quality Management (TQM) and has the four steps: Plan, Assess, Improve, Control. The approach focuses on the process that gives the results.

Total Productivity Management (TPM), World Class Manufacturing (WCM), and Lean Manufacturing follow an operational philosophy.

- TPM and its modern counterpart WCM have at their root the needs of Operations. In modern times, these have developed a holistic approach to the organizational needs, but their roots are still easily observable.

- I put Lean Manufacturing in this category as in part it tries to eliminate the problem through engineered solutions. In this sense the focus is Operations.

If we combine reliability and maintenance, we find that models such as PAS55 and its derivative ISO55000 try to reduce risk to meeting stakeholders' needs through a focus on strategy, organizational development and the evolution and application of the organization's technologies and asset management practices.

Ultimately, all of these philosophies and their resulting frameworks provide the same results: they just take different paths and words to get there. As managers and leaders, we need to identify which approach is best suited to our organization. We then need to properly communicate it in such a way as to not alienate the team members who would be more comfortable following other approaches. For the purpose of this book we will consider asset management as described by the PAS55/ISO55000 approach. We can then adapt this to the other approaches.

# World-Class Asset Management Business Process Elements

Maps are a helpful tool for defining and applying your business processes. In order to identify which elements to include in your business process maps, it is important to first identify the work groups that we are targeting. Many groups within your organization affect asset management. These mainly include: operations, maintenance, engineering, procurement and stores. You may wish to also include: human resources, safety, environment and training.

Once the target groups are identified we then define which processes these groups affect and therefore which processes to map. If we stick to the main work groups the selected asset management element maps may include the following:

- Developing a 3-year asset management strategy
- Facilities management
- Hierarchy development and management
- Analyzing risk and criticality
- Establishing asset performance targets
- Generating work requests
- Preventive maintenance (PM) optimization
- Reliability centered maintenance (RCM)
- Root cause failure analysis (RCFA)
- Managing modifications
- PM audit/review
- Implementing a PM task
- Configuring data collection in the computerized maintenance management system (CMMS)
- Managing the backlog

- Managing repairable spares
- Planning maintenance work
- Planning PMs
- Scheduling maintenance work
- Planning shutdowns
- Managing emergency and break-in work
- Executing maintenance work
- Managing work order follow-up
- Identifying and managing critical spare parts
- Managing bill of materials (BOM)
- Managing a kitting process
- Applying lifecycle costing
- Managing requisitions
- Generating a purchase order (PO)
- Expediting spare parts
- Receiving spare parts
- Returning spare parts to inventory
- Conducting inventory reviews and cycle counts
- Qualifying contractors and suppliers
- Managing operator routes
- Managing failure and defect reporting and elimination
- Conceptual engineering
- Design engineering
- Preliminary engineering
- Detailed engineering
- Commissioning and handover engineering projects

# Steps in Defining and Mapping the Business Process Elements

It is generally much easier to separate the business process into elements, and then to create a map for each element. Each element map is composed of tasks that represent the steps needed to properly support the element, and arrows to demonstrate their relationships. This is where we need to use judgment. How detailed we define the process will determine the usefulness of the map. A rule of thumb I like to use is that we want enough details so that the map becomes a good visual aid to do the work, but not so much detail as to render the map complex and difficult to use.

Some people use swim lanes as a way to depict who is responsible for each task. Swim lanes are typically horizontal zones where each zone represents a specific role within the organization. By looking at your lane you can easily see all tasks that are assigned to you. I like swim lanes if the maps are kept relatively simple, but on more complex maps the connecting lines are confusing. For more complex maps such as the ones discussed here, I prefer adding a header on each task to identify who is responsible for that task. The map then follows the process logically from start to finish and has sufficient details to be a useful visual aid.

When defining an element's process map, start by identifying the inputs and outputs of the element. Then, walk through the process step by step identifying the desired state – that is, how the element should be managed. To do this we need to involve the people who are currently part of the process. We also need a facilitator who understands best practices to guide the group.

In terms of process maps, many people start by mapping an element's current state and then move on to mapping its desired state. Unfortunately, most of the effort is spent on the current state maps, which will ultimately be thrown away. While we can use these to develop a migration path to desired state, there are much easier ways to do this, which we will discuss later. Incidentally, whenever I have mapped current state, I find that everyone is doing things his/her own way and there can be as many potential current state maps as there are individuals. I always go directly to desired state and have as yet not missed a beat.

The following are examples of process maps. As you will notice roles are added as headers and the maps follow the logical process steps. An important aspect of the maps is their visual value. We should always strive to document our processes and procedures and encourage/mandate our personnel to read and apply these. However, procedures tend to be wordy and cumbersome to refer to regularly. A graphical representation of the process, though not as thorough, is an excellent reinforcement tool and can easily be posted in strategic areas as a visual reminder.

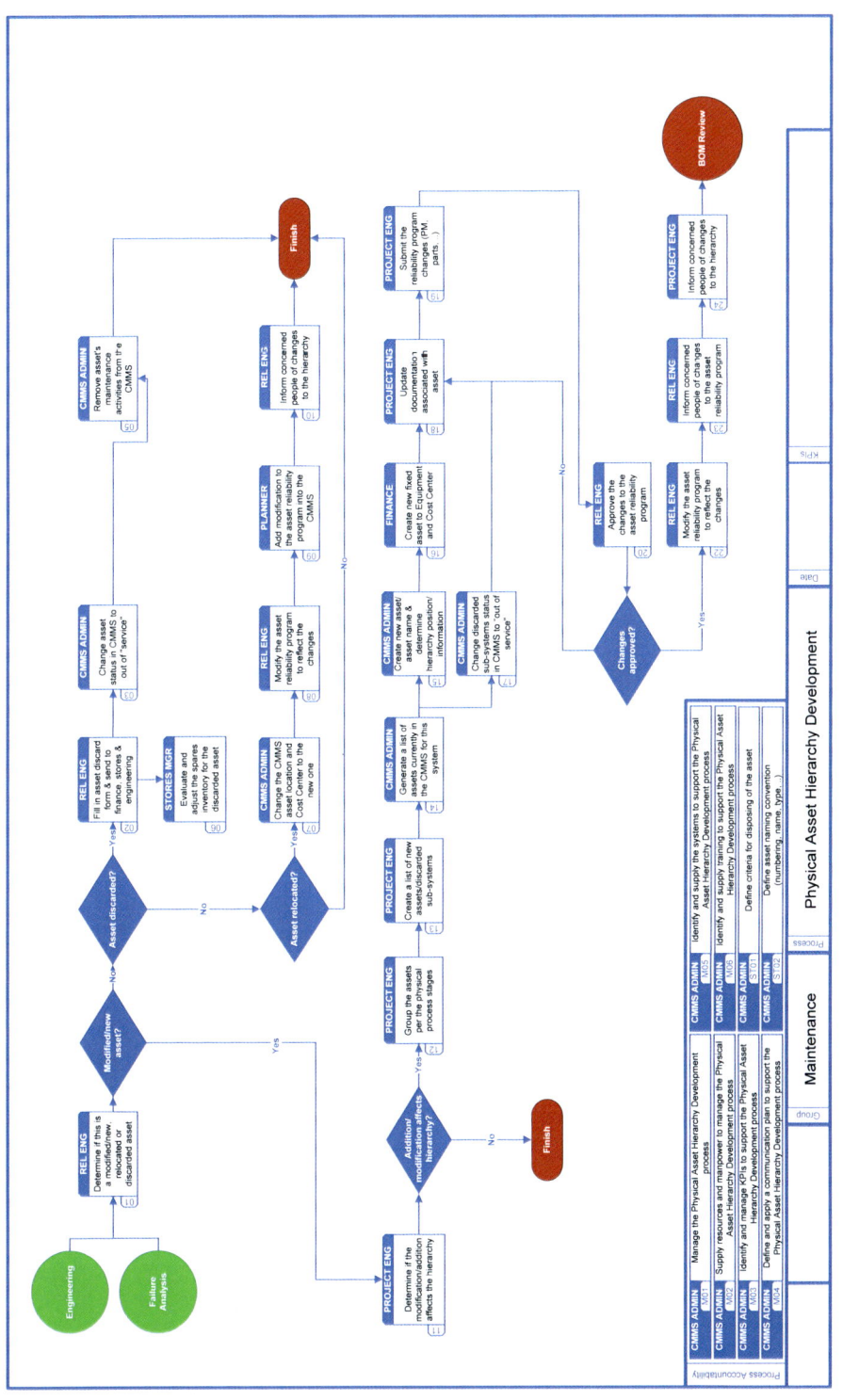

Map example

Asset Management Business Process

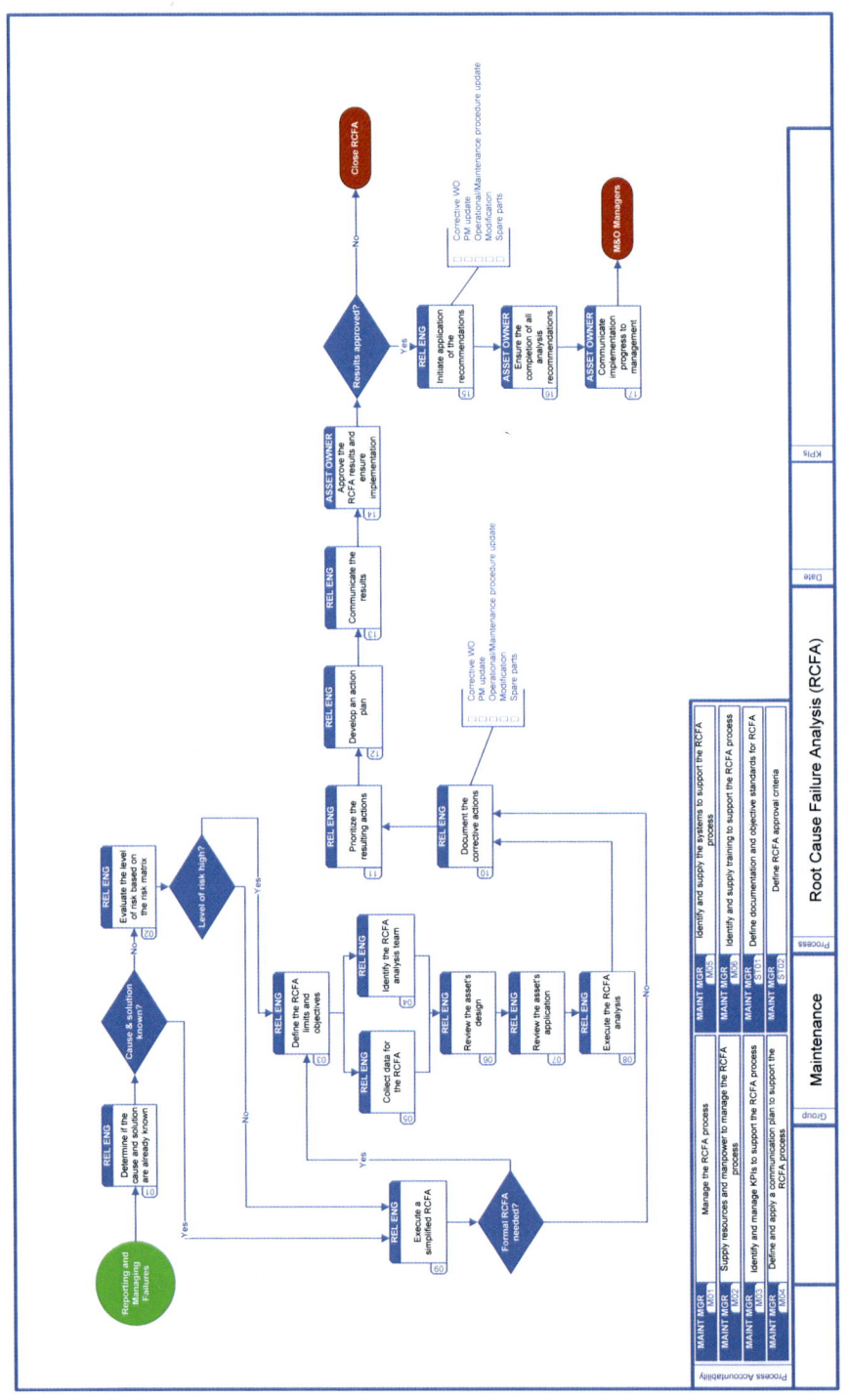

Map example

# Quality Measures

Once we have defined and mapped a business process we need to add quality measures. How do we know that a task is being done correctly? We tend to have a pretty good idea of what we mean by a task being done correctly but we rarely quantify and communicate it appropriately. As a result there is a lot of room for interpretation.

Whenever possible we should define a quality standard for each task in the process. Consider this task: "Review the backlog for jobs ready to plan." How do I know that this is being done correctly? Should this review be done daily, weekly? What criteria constitute a job ready to plan? Are these criteria being applied properly today?

It is also important to define exactly what we mean by "good" and to document this. As you may have gathered, this is not an easy task. It is actually quite difficult to describe what we mean by good, even though we expect our staff to do good work. This exercise serves two purposes: communicating quality standards to others and crystalizing those standards for ourselves.

The quality measures will then be used in business process deployment, which we will discuss in the section on Macro and Micro Deployment Strategies.

# A Better Approach to RACI

The next step is defining roles and responsibilities. RACI is a method used to identify every role that impacts – or is affected by – the task. The RACI process identifies who is responsible for the task (R); who is accountable (A), usually the responsible person's direct supervisor; who needs to be consulted (C) and who needs to be informed (I).

This concept has merit, but I have rarely seen it applied successfully. There are a number of reasons for this, one being the difficulty most people have in identifying who should be consulted and who should be informed. Another reason is the low value derived from assigning accountability at the task level.

I much prefer assigning accountability at the process, or element, level as we can therefore define the tasks needed to manage the process. In this way we assign responsibility at the task level (i.e. identify a job to plan) and accountability at the element level (i.e. planning a work order). For each map, the accountable person is responsible to manage the element, ensure the availability of resources, systems and tools, develop and manage a communication plan, and develop and track the KPIs that relate to this element.

This approach has a number of advantages. It provides a deployment and management structure, as well as management tasks that would not exist when assigning accountability at the task level with a conventional RACI process.

# Macro and Micro Deployment Strategies

It all comes down to deployment. Later in this book we will discuss how to manage and control the business process through meetings and KPIs. For now let us look at how to deploy the new roles in a practical way that produces results. The reason for developing the process maps and the roles and responsibilities is that we want to move from adapting our processes to the resources we have to adapting our resources to our best in class processes. Over the years, how we do things evolves as we continually adapt our practices to take advantage of strengths and compensate for weaknesses in our employees. This can make it difficult to hire new people to fill the roles, and introduces a myriad of inefficiencies of which we are sometimes unaware.

However, the problem is that while changing everything is overwhelming, everything is interlinked. So, if we only change some of the things we do we are probably causing even more problems.

The solution is actually quite simple: in a first phase, focus on aligning employees with their tasks and do not focus on the quality of the task execution, unless quality is a big issue. For example, you could ask the planner to list her current activities and compare this to the list of activities identified in the roles and responsibility mapping. Identify what is being done and what should not be done, and identify what new tasks should be done. Again, do not worry too much about task quality because that will come later. The first step is to realign tasks at the macro level.

The challenge to this strategy is most often getting individuals to stop doing certain tasks rather than getting them to add tasks to their list of responsibilities. Their reasoning is that if they do not do the task it will not be done or it will not be done right. These are often the same people who complain that they have too much to do.

It usually takes 6 to 12 months to render the new way of doing things into THE WAY of doing things. In other words, it takes this long to make this new system part of the organizational culture. Once this is accomplished, we are ready to focus on quality. This is where the task level quality measures come into play. You have the perfect audit tool as you have defined, at the task level, what 'good' looks like. Using these quality measures you can and should conduct audits one area at a time, and then use this information to define an action plan to address the shortfalls. This usually requires training and/or coaching.

A good and prudent first step to the quality audits, and even to the first phase, is to conduct a technical and soft skills assessment of the various resources. In this way you may discover that a person is not the right person for the job and may not benefit sufficiently from the training and coaching. Issues like this often become evident during the second phase of deployment but should be, if at all possible, identified and addressed during the first phase.

Finally, this is not a stagnant, one-time effort. The audit should be repeated periodically with training and coaching action plans developed and applied.

# Effective Staffing and Training

## The Role of Human Resources

Human Resources (HR) is tasked, or should be, with providing quality resources to the organization. This is achieved through its hiring and training practices, as well as through overseeing the management of these resources and introducing a personal performance measurement and development plan. HR is also responsible for attracting, selecting, training, assessing and rewarding employees.

In this chapter, we will discuss how to define the skills and abilities required to support the business process, and how to link these to the training and coaching curriculum. I believe that the caretaker of the overall business process maps and their supporting tools should be HR, as these define how we do business and provide the means to identify the human resources necessary for its support.

# Defining Skills and Abilities at the Task Level

In the previous chapter we discussed introducing quality measures at the task level. Once we have the tasks identified and quality measures defined for each task, we are in a position to be able to define the skills and abilities required to execute the task properly, to the required level of quality. For example, for the task "Review the backlog for jobs ready to plan," one of the skills required is a working knowledge of the computer maintenance management system (CMMS). Another is knowledge of the task selection criteria and how to apply them.

To record and manage this information, I recommend that you develop an ACCESS or SQL database. This will let you group and present the information in various ways, and it will help you communicate it to your co-workers. Also, as you develop the skills and abilities matrix you will notice that a number of tasks share the same skills and abilities. This is encouraging as the final list of skills and abilities per role is usually not overly long. A final review can help further group these in order to make the list manageable.

The specific skills and abilities defined for the tasks can eventually be grouped by roles and used as a basis for conducting a skills assessment of the individuals responsible for filling these roles. This provides a much more relevant skills evaluation matrix, aligned with your business model.

# Task-Specific Training and Coaching

With a clear understanding of the skills and abilities necessary to execute the task at the desired level of quality, we are well positioned to identify the training and coaching tools required to develop these skills. The training and coaching tools should be defined at the task level and entered into the previously mentioned database. As with the defined skills and abilities, the list per role is not particularly long.

Interestingly, there is growing evidence in neurological rehabilitation of the value of task specific training for people who have suffered traumas such as strokes. A clear and specific list of tasks, repeated many times over helps the body relearn its neural pathways and reestablish lost motor skills. Though I am in no way equating your employees to stroke victims we can learn from this example. By clearly defining the training, rather than the traditional shotgun approach we can more quickly achieve the desired performance levels and, in so doing, not confuse people with unnecessary information and training.

During my discussions with site personnel a common concern is the lack of training. Further research usually shows that the organization gives quite a bit of training and the real issues are not the amount of training but the relevance of the training programs to the needs of the individual, perceived or real. Task specific training resolves many of these issues.

# Developing a Training Program

Once the training and coaching requirements are defined, these can be grouped and compared to the existing curriculum. This usually provides much needed information to the Training Department so that they can adjust the curriculum of existing courses and identify additional course requirements. An organization I know uses a SQL server to record the tasks, quality standards, skills and abilities and training and coaching requirements and linked these back to the roles and individuals. Individual credentials and certifications were added and refresher frequencies identified for specific courses. Finally, the database allows them to record skill gaps, based on the quality audits, and link these to specific remedial training activities.

Once the training needs are established and these are compared to existing curriculums you should convene representatives of the affected workgroups to review and validate the new courses. Easy, low cost options should be considered and practical training plans developed.

In a world-class environment, 5 percent of the maintenance man-hours are spent in training. I am not certain of the percentage for other roles but it is probably similar. Training departments are tasked with providing training and are often frustrated by the lack of input into this training as well as the low attendance. To become world-class we need to train our people, but with the right training. The approach recommended in this book will ensure that the training is aligned with your business model. It will help you develop role-specific training curriculums as well as person-specific training. This approach will also help you measure the results of the training through the quality audits.

# Improving the Training Program

Your business, the tools you use, and your understanding of how you should be conducting business are constantly evolving. This is a dynamic environment and your business processes need to evolve to adapt to change if you want to continue to be successful. This evolution will lead to new requirements for your training and coaching programs.

Even if you do not change your business process documentation some of your people will change how they do things to adjust to the perceived new needs. I use the word perceived as not all changes will be necessary or even welcomed but if you do not stay on top of the process you will be unable to manage the evolution and will fall back into a people dependency mode.

It is human nature to want to change things and it will be a constant challenge to make certain that everyone does things the right way. If your processes are wrong due to changes in your business, and you know they are wrong, it will be difficult to insist on people following them. To a certain extent this is okay, but how can you conduct a quality control program when you know your standards are wrong? Furthermore, how can you have an effective training program when your training curriculum is not aligned with how you do business?

Therefore, it is important to develop a review structure for your formalized business processes and their supporting information (performance attributes and required skills and abilities). This same process should also review the training curriculum and make adjustments as needed, including an evergreen training process to inform and train employees on changes in your business model. The review should be conducted yearly.

Another source of change, hopefully, is that your organization will use this process to mature in its understanding and application of best practices. As your organization matures you will become more severe in your interpretation of quality and will require a higher level of performance from your employees. These changes must also be incorporated into your training program.

# Effective Staffing

Staffing is an ongoing challenge for many organizations as they try to improve or maintain the company's performance while facing budget cuts, attritions, hiring freezes and limitations in the current staff's skills and abilities. Effective staffing is assured through training, hiring practices and management techniques that are aligned with the organization's business process. This will in turn make the organization more system dependent rather than people dependent and provide the structure to weather the storm when there are changes in personnel or in company direction.

In this chapter we described how to extrapolate training and coaching requirements from the process maps. These same maps will also provide a specific technical component of the job description for the specific role. For example, once every task has been assigned to a role it is quite simple to group the tasks by roles, providing a good – though incomplete – job description. The addition of soft skills and non-asset management related tasks make the job description complete.

It is important to note that different organizations have different needs. For example a 6-man maintenance crew will have different needs that a 200-man maintenance crew. Actually, they all have the same needs but we meet them somewhat differently. For example, the 6-man crew will not have enough work to justify separate Planners and Schedulers while the 200-man crew most certainly can justify different resources and may even have a Planning/Scheduling Supervisor and a Shutdown Coordinator.

The advantage of using the maps to assign roles to tasks is that you can partition these in many different ways. For example you may decide to create a Planner Level 1 and a Planner Level 2. Depending on the needs of your organization you can then assign a role to a person or a group of people or assign multiple roles to one person. The process does not change but how you apply it is different. This helps you model a staffing structure that is effective for your organization. In the end it really does not matter how you group tasks and roles as long as each task is executed to the right level of quality.

In this section I refer to skills that are specific to the asset management process. An effective staff also requires technical skills. For example mechanics need to know their trade and will also need specialized knowledge on the equipment being maintained. A skills assessment should be conducted to evaluate these skills.

Once the role is properly defined and gaps identified, effective staffing techniques can be used to address gaps in your organization's ability to respond to business strategies and changes. Your staffing strategy should also define what the organization should do to eliminate or reduce staffing gaps and surpluses.

By deploying a flexible and cost-effective approach to staffing, organizations can better manage their resource pool, maintaining service levels and minimizing costs. The first step is to develop a staffing plan. This plan considers the short and long term needs of the organization and includes contingency plans to address volatilities in your work levels. The contingencies may, and usually should, include the use of temporary resources in order to prevent over hiring. These temporary resources will help deal with short-term personnel gaps, specialized knowledge requirements and special projects.

# Efficient Meetings

## Why Do Meetings Fail?

We should manage our business process with meetings and control it with KPIs.

Typically, our meetings and KPIs are only loosely linked to our business process and do not produce the desired results. In most organizations I have visited over the years the common theme is that we have too many meetings, and that these usually drag on with little results. People show up unprepared, many people are late, there is no agenda, or if there is one it is not followed…

The number of complaints regarding meetings seems endless, even though it should not be difficult to organize and facilitate a meeting. Why do we have these problems? There are a number of reasons, and I am certain that there are a few I have not included in this book. One simple reason is that we are too busy to take the time to properly structure our meetings. Another reason is that we assume that everyone understands the purpose and structure of the meeting, even though we rarely create an agenda, or follow it if there is one. Another reason is the meeting's value or lack thereof, perceived or real. This perception rises mainly because of a lack of planning on the part of the leadership team. Finally, when the meeting is boring people do not want to attend and find ways to bail out physically or mentally.

For boring meetings, you have to first understand what makes the meeting boring, and ultimately unproductive. Then you can work towards making the meeting interesting, rather than a chore. During a boring meeting, the participant mentally checks out of the meeting before it even starts. To solve this have issues to resolve, develop action plans, follow up on action plans, etc. In other words do something productive. Use the meeting to keep everyone in the loop, but do not meet so often that there is rarely any progress to report.

However, you might want to consider shorter, more frequent meetings where specific topics are reviewed at specific meetings to keep the meetings interesting and productive. Schedule set days and times for each type of meeting so that everyone knows what to expect and when. People will be more prepared and ready to deliver when the time comes.

In this chapter, we will explore the mechanics of good meetings. This includes:

- A review of a good meeting structure;

- Defining simple and practical solutions to meetings. Simply reducing the number of meetings, as some organizations are trying to do, is not the solution;

- A review of the four types of meetings;

- Discussing how to map meetings to better understand their interrelationships and purpose within the asset-management process;

- Options for auditing the meetings.

# Structuring Your Meetings

Step one in solving the inefficiency of your meetings is to structure them. Step two is to follow the structure. I like developing a practices document for the meeting, which includes:

## Meeting Purpose

This is a simple, sentence-length explanation of why we have the meeting in the first place. It essentially becomes the vision of the team participating in the meeting.

# Responsible

The person responsible is different than the facilitator. It is not unusual for the role of facilitator to rotate among the participants, which is an excellent approach. There needs to be a person with overall and permanent responsibility and accountability for the meeting to ensure that the meeting stays true to its purpose.

# Participants

As mentioned previously, it is not unusual to have too many participants identified and to have irregular participation. Select the participants carefully and only include those who must be there. Participation is then mandatory. I tend to dislike adding someone to the list as optional because this is too often an excuse to miss the meeting. They either need to be there or not. This does not mean that someone else cannot occasionally audit the meeting or come in for a specific topic. Also, it is usually better to document the person's title rather than their name, when defining the meeting parameters, as people tend to change roles over the years.

# Information Required for the Meeting

Too often we show up for a meeting unprepared, or vital information is missing, and we waste time trying to recreate this information from memory, leading to wrong decisions. Pre-meeting preparation is crucial to efficient and effective meetings. Define upfront the information required for the meeting and task someone to produce it prior to the meeting. This information falls into two categories: information we always need for the meeting and information identified during a previous meeting for review during this meeting.

# Meeting Deliverables

This is different from Meeting Purpose as it is not about explaining why the meeting exists but rather listing the expected outcomes of the meeting.

# Agenda

It is important to have topics for discussion include who is responsible for each topic and how much time is allotted to the topic. While there is sometimes a need to introduce a new topic for the meeting, a standard agenda helps people come in more prepared and will lead to an overall efficiency gain in the meeting. We may not always be able to follow the proposed timeline but the closer we stay on topic and on schedule, the better the meeting will flow and people will be more enthusiastic regarding participation.

# Meeting Logistics

This includes such things as meeting location, when it occurs, frequency and even which business process the meeting manages.

## Meeting Category

The meeting category is an interesting tool to use as it helps us question, in a structured way, the purpose of the meeting. It also helps us ensure value. A meeting may fulfill more than one category but if it is meant to fulfill too many categories, this may be a sign that the meeting definition is flawed and should be partitioned into more than one meeting.

The meeting purpose categories include:

- Consult – Expert input is required.

- Discuss – People's input is required, not necessarily as experts.

- Action Plan – The meeting is designed to define actions, usually following a specific activity or analysis.

- Inform – This meeting is a communication tool. Be careful, as this is not the most efficient way to communicate. Instead, you may wish to use other communication tools such as communication boards and emails.

- Control – This type of meeting is usually used to review specific activities or actions and to manage their progress.

## Annual Cost of Meetings

I always find it interesting to calculate the annual cost of the meeting and then compare this to the projected value. Annual cost is simply the number of hours in meetings per year times the number of participants times the weighted annual salary of the individuals. This helps clarify the value of adding certain individuals to the meeting, as well as the value of the frequency chosen.

## Meeting Standards

It never hurts to define meeting standards and remind people of these standards on a regular basis. This helps prevent the meeting from degenerating into something less than the ideal. The following are some of the standards that you may wish to use:

| MEETING STANDARDS | |
|---|---|
| On time, follow agenda, cellphone and pager off | Respect others without bias |
| Presence is required with a backup plan when needed | All are equal and invited to participate |
| I am prepared, I listen and I participate | I am committed and I deliver |
| Open, honest and impersonal discussions | All ideas are good ideas |

# The Four Types of Meetings

There are four types of meetings:

- Strategic
- Systemic
- Situational
- Ad Hoc

Each meeting type has a different focus and structure and involves different people in the organization. Without a clear understanding of the meeting type, there is a possibility (certainty in many cases) that the wrong resources will be present. Often, we tend to add too many resources to our meetings, just in case, costing the organization valuable time.

## Strategic Meetings
These meetings are used to set the direction and scope of the organization over the long term. They are also used to develop and manage these strategies in order to meet corporate and site objectives. These meetings are typically held annually, bi-annually or quarterly.

Strategic meetings are often held off-site to help employees remove themselves from the business, physically and mentally. They are used to establish or reevaluate strategy and discuss performance.

## Systemic Meetings
These meetings are used to identify and manage the systems and processes used to support the strategies. During these meetings, we review progress of the systems and processes and provide direction to the organization. These meetings are typically held quarterly or monthly.

Systemic meetings are used to discuss major issues and big topics – whatever has a long-term effect on the business. These meetings encourage discussions and debate where people can present new ideas.

## Situational Meetings
During these meetings we identify and follow up on activities that support the systems and processes. We use these meetings to track progress, provide direction and adapt as needed. These meetings are held weekly, daily or even every shift.

These meetings include daily quick check-ins, which are usually short and to the point. They are used to get updates, assign daily tasks and address concerns. Weekly meetings are tactical in nature and allow people to focus on what is immediately important.

## Ad-Hoc Meetings

These meetings are used to address specific goals and activities that are not included in the situational meetings. These meetings are usually singular or temporary in nature. If there is a need to make an ad-hoc meeting permanent it should be incorporated in an existing situational meeting, or a new situational meeting should be created.

Ad-hoc meetings are useful and necessary, but they can also be used to compensate for poor meetings or to circumvent the process. You should always question the purpose of the ad-hoc meeting and determine if changes are needed so that this meeting can be eliminated in the future.

In the next section we discuss mapping meetings. Ad-hoc meetings are not included in this mapping.

# Meeting Maps

Similarly to the business processes, there is value in mapping the interrelationships between meetings, as each type of meeting has a purpose. As discussed previously, the situational meetings are there to manage the activities that support the systems and programs that are developed to support the strategies we defined. The systemic meetings of course are there to manage the systems and programs. The strategic meetings exist to develop and manage the strategies we developed, in order to support the organizational policies. Thus, each type of meeting must be cognizant of the meeting that is supporting it, or of the meeting that it is supporting. A clear understanding of these interrelationships helps better define the deliverables of each meeting and ultimately its true purpose and helps communicate this information to the participants.

I tend to be visual by nature and find that creating maps of the meetings not only helps me understand how they fit together, but it also helps me communicate this to others. I also like to separate the meeting maps by departments such as Production, Maintenance, Engineering and Management.

Earlier in this book I mentioned that I usually do not like the swim lane approach because business process maps are too complex. However, when

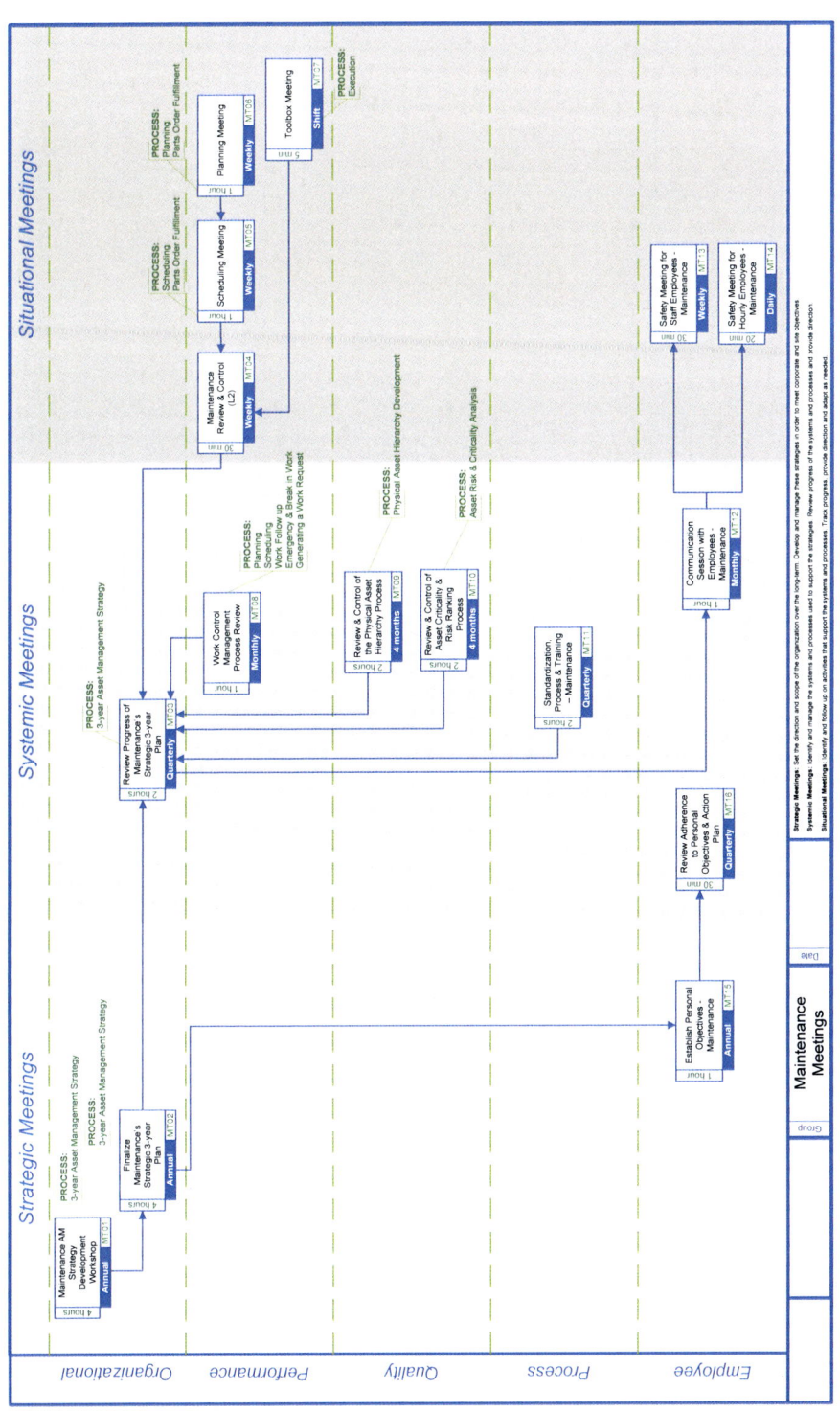

Efficient Meetings 25

it comes to mapping meetings, I prefer swim lanes because the maps are relatively simple and the swim lane approach provides great visual information. If you find that your maps are complex, you most likely have too many meetings and should consider eliminating some.

On the previous page is an example of a meeting map with swim lanes. You will notice that we created swim lanes in both directions. Vertical lanes are for the types of meetings and horizontal lanes are for the overall function of the meeting. We also added a callout for each box to identify the business process map associated with the meeting, gave each meeting a unique number, and added duration and frequency components to each meeting.

As you can see, with the map it is easy to understand how the meeting fits into the overall structure. Any missing or redundant meetings also become clear. I find that this type of map lets us quickly see if the meeting is in the right category, especially when you consider meeting frequency.

# Auditing Meetings to Ensure Effectiveness and Efficiency

You have developed each meeting's format, made certain that you have just the right number of meetings, the right people are present, and that the meetings provide value. Now you need to deploy the new meetings and ensure sustainability. My preferred approach is to define exactly what is meant by 'good' and to communicate this to the participants. To do this, I like to add a self-audit to the meeting practice document. The following is an example. Usually each requirement is weighted according to its importance to the efficiency of the meeting.

Once the participants have attended a few meetings, it is good practice to periodically bring in an external auditor to review the meetings, using the same standards as the self-audit.

# SELF AUDIT

| REQUIREMENT | YES | NO |
|---|---|---|
| **ADHERENCE** (meeting practices) | | |
| Meeting starts on time | | |
| Meeting finishes on time | | |
| Agenda published and distributed before the meeting | | |
| No one is surprised by the agenda and subjects discussed | | |
| Agenda is followed | | |
| Everyone scheduled is present | | |
| **COMMUNICATION** (I listen and I participate) | | |
| Discussions between certain members before the meeting help efficiently resolve subjects that would normally require too much discussion during the meeting | | |
| The subjects discussed are included in the agenda | | |
| Meeting objectives were communicated prior to the meeting | | |
| Discussions are encouraged but controlled in order to respect the schedule and ensure everyone's participation | | |
| The participants are prepared and able to participate in the topics discussed | | |
| Deviations are controlled and minimized | | |
| Everyone participates in the discussions at the appropriate moments | | |
| **ENGAGEMENT** (identification of barriers, assignments and resolutions) | | |
| Assigned actions are reviewed and their schedule respected | | |
| When needed a task is reassigned but with a shortened timeline | | |
| Shortfalls in the action plans are questioned and corrective actions are identified | | |
| All relevant actions are reviewed and assigned to specific resources | | |
| All assigned actions have a due date | | |
| Assigned dates are reviewed to ensure the right level of urgency | | |
| All assigned tasks are reviewed prior to closing the meeting | | |
| **FEEDBACK** (celebrate our successes and focus on the problems) | | |
| Successes are recognized during the meeting | | |
| Weak performances are identified and reviewed in order to bridge the gap | | |
| **TOTAL** | | |

# Effective Key Performance Indicators

## KPIs as Value Focusing Tools

Most organizations put significant importance and effort in developing KPIs. Some call these 'goals' and others 'objectives.' Yet many find it difficult to quantify benefits achieved by the use of these same KPIs. In some cases we develop KPIs because management told us to, and management wants KPIs because world-class organizations have KPIs. We do what we can to attain the defined targets and deep down recognize their importance but we are somehow unable to derive the desired benefits from them.

"If you can't measure it you can't manage it." (Peter Drucker) However, the reverse is not necessarily true: even if you can measure it does not guarantee that you can manage it. KPIs are essential tools to measuring organizational performance. In order to use these to manage performance it is important to carefully select the right KPIs and systemize the process in which they are used.

KPIs can be defined as quantifiable measurements that reflect the critical success factors of the organization. They help organizations achieve their goals through the definition and measurement of progress. Performance measurement is a fundamental principle of management. It is important because it identifies performance gaps between current and desired performance, as well as providing an indication of progress towards closing these gaps. Carefully selected KPIs identify precisely where to take action to improve performance, providing a valuable focusing tool.

As mentioned above, some organizations use the terms 'goals' or 'objectives' rather than 'KPI.' In essence these are the same, but they do have different connotations. The term Key Performance Indicator implies a scientific, measurable and performance-based method, while goals and objectives tend to imply a more human-focused measure. Because words are so important in communicating what we are trying to achieve, you should take a moment to decide which term to use in your organization. For the purpose of this chapter, we will use the term KPI throughout, as this is applicable to goals and objectives.

# Normalizing Our Definitions

Before developing KPIs we need to agree on definitions. Variations between organizations – and even within organizations – regarding definitions create confusion and misinterpretations. Most people tend to choose definitions that support their approach and provide a positive result from a KPI point of view. This is difficult to change as no one wants to look bad, yet in order to be successful, we must adopt clear KPIs and KPI definitions that are universally accepted.

In my opinion, the best source for definitions is the Society of Maintenance and Reliability Professionals (SMRP) at www.smrp.org. This is not to say that SMRP has defined every useful KPI, or that I agree with every KPI that they have defined, but the definitions that they have developed are sound and can be used as references.

# KPI Categories

Some KPIs are used to track results (e.g. reportable earnings), while others are used to control or govern a process (e.g. percentage of maintenance work orders that are planned). These can be separated into two categories: leading and lagging KPIs.

## Leading KPIs

In project management, leading metrics are forward-looking. For example: Projected program finish date based upon the rate of milestone completion.

In asset management, leading KPIs are measurements focused on the process that is used to achieve the results, or on the organization that produces the results. A leading KPI could be: Percentage completed work orders with all required information.

## Lagging KPIs

In project management, lagging indicators are most valuable for a retrospective view of program performance. For example: Percentage deliverables completed.

In asset management, lagging indicators are results focused measurements: Cost per ton or Number of tons produced per day.

We cannot affect the results (lagging KPIs); we can only try to do better next time. However, from a shareholder perspective results are the ultimate goal of the organization. These include safety, environmental and operational objectives.

I find that people often have difficulties distinguishing between leading and lagging KPIs. Let's look at this example: My daughter drives a car and I track the number of accidents she gets into every year. We undoubtedly have long discussions about this but other than her promising to do better next year, nothing can be done to change the past or improve our insurance rates for this year. The number of accidents is a lagging indicator. This is important from a financial perspective, but we cannot change the number of accidents.

Let's say that I was watching her drive and noticed that she does not signal before turning. Does not signaling guarantee that she will get into an accident? Of course not. If she always signals, will the number of accidents per year decrease? Yes. Therefore, if I monitor her driving habits, such as signaling, and encourage good habits, the number of accidents will drop, hopefully to zero. Her habits are leading indicators. Doing something wrong once does not guarantee bad results but if everything is done right all the time the likelihood of good results is high.

In simple terms, leading KPIs are measures of the habits and behavior of our workforce and lagging KPIs are measures of the results of those same habits and behaviors. In order to achieve favorable results we have to focus on the habits and behaviors as measured by the leading KPIs.

Despite this, it can sometimes be difficult to distinguish between leading and lagging KPIs as most KPIs have children contributors. For example, workforce efficiency is affected by how well we plan and schedule work and by the skill level of the workers. The skill level of the workers is affected by our hiring and training practices. How well we plan work is influenced by the presence of standard job plans, bills of materials (BOMs), and the ratio of planners to tradespeople. Most people consider all of these metrics as leading (process) KPIs and they can be used to impact behavior, if measured and communicated properly.

Depending on the time measurement scale, many process KPIs can act as results KPIs, challenging your ability to affect change. If we go back to the car example, say that I develop statistics on the percentage of times my daughter signals before turning. This is an interesting leading KPI, but say that I publish my findings once every ten years. Though this is a leading KPI it is unlikely that I will be able to use the information to influence behavior. In effect, the KPI acts more like a lagging than a leading KPI due to the communication frequency.

Our goal is to measure so that we can control and manage our process. It is therefore to our benefit to choose time scales that are practical, and that provide as much leading indication as possible, without overburdening our organization.

To consistently achieve the desired results, we need to influence the process that leads to the results. For example, if the percentage of work orders planned drops, then the maintenance department's short-term performance may or may not be significantly affected, but in the long term the maintenance team will be less efficient. This impacts team performance, and ultimately impacts plant performance and shareholder earnings.

# Assuring Results

Results can only be assured and sustained by focusing on the process that delivers the results, that is, on the leading indicators. This is at the root of effective KPI development. We too often look at the results, congratulate ourselves or not on these and, when the results are negative, try to do better next time. This is all without an achievable plan in place. Sustainable results require a plan and this plan must focus on what we can affect: the process or organization that gave us the results. The process or organization is measured using leading KPIs.

Where organizations often have problems is when there is no clear correlation between the results metrics (lagging KPIs) and the process metrics (leading KPIs). In other words, the effects are not linked to their causes. As our focus tends to be on the results, and we cannot change these results, we are doomed to repeating the same mistakes with little to no improvement. Deming once said: "Your systems [and processes] are perfectly designed for the results you are getting." We need to change our process in order to get different results. In terms of KPIs, we need to focus on the leading KPIs so as to improve our lagging KPIs. But we also need to define and quantify the relationship between the leading and lagging KPIs so that each leading KPI's value is properly defined and communicated.

Proper planning around the KPIs is another important factor. It is not enough to define objectives: we also need to understand what we are trying to achieve, align the KPIs with the desired benefits and make certain that we can manage our process using these KPIs in order to achieve the desired benefits.

Selecting the right number of KPIs is also essential. A common problem with KPIs is that every group wants their own and organizations end up creating too many KPIs. Some organizations have tried to resolve this dilemma by creating one global KPI that embodies all of the KPIs. This is something akin to an organizational health indicator whereby a single measure provides indication of the organization's performance. The simplicity and elegance of the solution is brilliant, but it creates its own set of problems.

The major issue with the above-mentioned solution is that a gain in one KPI may camouflage a loss in another KPI. Presumably, people are managing at the KPI level and these issues will be addressed. This said, visibility at the executive level may be lost and consequently, sponsorship to resolve the shortcomings may be more difficult to secure.

I am not opposed to an organizational health indicator and in fact there are real benefits to developing one. Before beginning, you must ensure that the word "key" in KPI is well understood and applied. Once only the "key" indicators have been defined, and proper steps are in place to manage based on these, then you are in a position to consider a health indicator.

# Applying KPIs to Performance Management Plans

A proper selection of effective KPIs provides the tools needed to define individual staff objectives and Performance Management Plans (PMP). (These are also called: Performance Management and Development, Performance Development Plan, or Performance Management System.) Usually a PMP structure is developed corporately and deployed at the plant level. The PMPs reflect the plant's operating plan as it relates to corporate objectives. Targets and goals typically fall in the following categories: Productivity, Quality, Cost, Delivery, Safety and Morality (PQCDSM).

PMPs can be effective if they focus on what people can affect, in other words, if they focus on leading KPIs. Therefore, the right leading KPIs must be defined, following rules recommended in this chapter, and properly deployed to make these meaningful to a PMP program.

# Rules for Defining KPIs

## Performance Management and KPIs

Maintaining workforce performance and productivity levels is more important than ever in our competitive marketplace. Unfortunately we are faced with retirements, difficulty in finding skilled workers and a need to keep costs down, leading to lean workforces.

It is difficult but the organizations that achieve the highest success with their performance management process are those who invest in their employees, involve their employees in the decision process, have strong leadership, and deploy well-executed communication plans. When properly applied, performance management helps ensure a stable, happy and productive workforce.

Well-defined and applied KPIs are an essential part of a performance management program. This is because a KPI program requires strong leadership and vision to develop, involves the employees in the decision process, and is part of a well-executed communication and personal-management performance plan.

# Purpose of Lagging KPIs

Lagging KPIs measure results and provide indication of the organization or group's adherence to the stakeholders' stated requirements. By 'stakeholders' we are referring to the shareholders, employees and society as a whole. As such, the various classes of Lagging KPIs are listed in the pneumonic PQCDSM:

- **P**roductivity
- **Q**uality
- **C**ost
- **D**elivery
- **S**afety
- **M**oral

We also add environmental adherence to the list.

Specific examples of Lagging KPIs are included in the Physical Asset Management Example KPIs section of this book.

When defining lagging KPIs, limit the number of KPIs to those that are attainable and that have real meaning to the organization, employees and society.

# Purpose of Leading KPIs

It is always interesting to discuss the purpose of leading KPIs with people. Leading KPIs are indicators of the process or organization that leads to the results. Organizations are comprised of people, therefore leading KPIs are tools used to encourage people to do things a certain way in order to achieve the desired results. Ultimately, leading KPIs influence the behavior of individuals and groups by identifying, measuring and communicating specifics of the process where performance is important to the sustained success of the organization. The behavior we wish to influence needs to be clearly articulated, and the positive and negative results of this behavior identified.

It is important to describe both the positive and negative impact of the metric you wish to introduce, as it may be that the negative impact outweighs the positive.

For example, sports teams and leagues often develop new rules or systems in order to either win more games or make the product more entertaining. Too often the negatives that also ensue overshadow the benefits achieved by the change. This is evidenced in North American ice hockey where the centerline has been removed to speed up the game. With relatively small ice surfaces and bigger players, the increased speed has contributed to an increase in the number of concussions.

## Beliefs and Behaviors

At this point we need to discuss the relationship between beliefs and behaviors and their impact on sustainability. You can force people to behave a certain way but our natural tendency is to behave in such a way as to support our beliefs. For example, if I believe that walking under a ladder will definitely bring me bad luck I will do everything in my power to go around the ladder. If I'm ordered to always pass under the ladder I will do so to keep my job but will stop doing so once pressure to adhere to the rule is lowered.

However, if we influence people's belief system we will create a situation where their natural tendency will be to behave as desired, which will result in sustainability. The best place to start is by answering the question: "What's in it for me." If the person sees that he will benefit from positively affecting the results of the KPI it is more likely that he will behave accordingly. By benefiting I do not mean that his boss will be happy but rather that these results will make his job easier, increase the organization's financial performance, which will create job security, or he will gain in another way.

In the book *The Little Prince*, the main character met a king who was a despot. Every command he gave was followed to the letter without question. When asked by the little prince how he could be assured that his commands would always be followed the king told him that this was easy: he never told people to do something that they did not wish to do. The same is true with KPIs. By first defining and communicating the benefits the person will derive from the KPI, it will be much easier to implement and ensure long-term sustainability.

## Negative Impact of Not Achieving the KPI

We also need to understand and quantify, if possible, the negative impact of not achieving the KPI. If there is no negative impact, then why do we have the KPI in the first place?

An example of this is a meeting I had with a production facility. The maintenance and reliability group was mandated to increase asset availability, a worthy objective. While equipment availability was much lower than desired, the facility's productivity targets were always met. Therefore, from an operations perspective there is no negative impact of not achieving the availability target. As a result, the yearly equipment availability KPI was never met and never will be. Nor should it be, unless we can clearly identify and communicate a negative impact of not achieving the KPI. In this case it may be the excessive use of energy and labor. Further, if we cannot identify a negative impact then the KPI should be removed.

This example serves to bring up an important point. We must clearly define and articulate the benefit of a KPI (what is in it for me?) at every level. For a behavior-targeted KPI (leading) to be most effective it is important for those whose behavior we want to affect to see a benefit.

## Reviewing KPI with Targeted Resources

The people whose behavior the KPI is targeting should be informed and have a chance to influence the KPI. They may or may not be allowed to change the KPI, especially if this is mandated by corporate, but they should be invited to define how to meet the targets. This will ferret out any errors in the plan and develop ownership on their part. In turn, this will greatly increase the probability of successfully achieving the KPI's objective.

## Selecting an Owner

The owner must not only be responsible for the success of the KPI, they must be empowered (by the organization) to take all reasonable action to meet and sustain the desired target.

Responsibility for this KPI is typically part of the person's performance management plan (PMP). Accountability for the KPI on the other hand should be part of the person's supervisor's PMP.

## Selecting a Target

When selecting a target, be careful to select one that will lead to the desired outcome, all the while being attainable. It is perfectly acceptable to challenge people, but too aggressive a challenge tends to have an adverse affect on behavior. On the other hand, if current performance is abysmal then it may be necessary to map out a transition plan to get from where we are currently to reaching our goal.

For example, let us say that the maintenance organization is only 20 percent proactive. You may be aware that world-class organizations are somewhere in the neighborhood of 80 to 85 percent proactive. Setting a target of 80 percent proactive will not guarantee that the target will be achieved. An understanding of why the organization is at 20% proactive is necessary, as well as an initiative to correct whatever needs to be corrected. As progress is made the target should gradually be increased, at an aggressive but attainable rate, until the final objective is met.

This brings us to another point: what is 'world class'? Knowing what is possible and what has been possible for others helps us set realistic goals as well as realistic ideals. We frequently see this in sports when seemingly impossible feats (e.g. 100 meters sprint under 10 seconds) are achieved. Within a few years they become commonplace and new, impossible targets are being set (e.g. 100 meters in under 9.8 seconds).

It is important to keep in mind that world class is not a specific target, but rather the best of the best. Once a target is met someone will beat it, setting up a new world-class target. To be world class means that you are forever striving to improve on your own accomplishments.

Of course you will think that while a target was met in that particular organization or industry, things are different at your organization. You may be entirely correct, but with this mindset you may actually be limiting your potential. The one truism I've run into in industries all over the world is that though things are different in your organization, organizations are more similar than dissimilar and they tend to share the same kinds of challenges.

I mentioned world class but we should also discuss best in class. Best in class takes into account the variations between regions, industries and the state of your organization. Best in class may be more suitable for your needs but you should be careful, as this can be an excuse to not improve. World-class organizations do not limit themselves to their industry alone and learn from all industries and regions to constantly improve.

Whichever model you are using, the information required to set targets is usually acquired through benchmarking exercises. This can be difficult to orchestrate, since those to which we need to compare ourselves – if they have similar conditions as we have – may very well be our competitors. Benchmarking exercises also tend be expensive, and can sometimes be substituted with a ready-made assessment database.

Whether you use world-class or best-in-class data, the key point is that it is important to know what 'good' looks like. This will help develop a realistic vision and fuel the drive to improve. After all, if others are able to achieve these results then so should you.

## Measurement Environment

For a KPI to be effective, the information must be correct, accurate and believable. Also, there must not be any lapses in data. To ensure this, the tool used to measure and track the KPI must be as automated as possible, definitions well understood and the information easily accessible.

A glossary of terms and formulae should be developed and communicated, and a software environment used to track and display the KPIs. The software should be linked to the various sources of information so that no (or few) manual entries are necessary. The use of electronic dashboards help keep all involved informed of the results.

## Developing a Communication Plan

We said that the purpose of a leading KPI is to influence behavior. In order to do so, we must keep the people whose behavior we are influencing informed about the status of the KPI.

When meeting people from various organizations, a common theme is that their respective companies do a poor job of communicating. In most cases, what I have observed is not a lack of communication, but the wrong communication. Too much wrong information is being communicated and vital information is all but impossible to separate out. We fill each square inch of our dashboards with data and we measure and communicate many performance indicators, usually lagging.

To resolve these issues, a good KPI development and deployment strategy needs a communication plan. This includes:

## Defining the Audience

Who is the KPI meant for? How does this person or group prefer to communicate? The audience may be comprised of many different groups at various levels of the organization. Each group may have unique communication needs.

It is important to identify each target group and person, as well as particularities concerning them (e.g. how they like to communicate, any sensitive issues). Do not get carried away. Too many people, like too many KPIs, will confuse things and reduce the effectiveness of the KPI.

If the leading KPI is there to influence behavior, it is important to identify whose behavior we want to influence, and to make certain that they are included in the communication plan.

## Defining Goals

With stated objectives, and considering available human and financial resources, define goals. In other words, there needs to be a program of work for each objective. Goals include general programs, products or services that you will use to achieve stated objectives. For example, if the objective is to improve percentage of work requests with sufficient information, the solution might include improved training for those generating work requests, special communications directed at first-time requestors, a reference sheet on how to fill in a work request, and ongoing information for those who are tasked with generating work requests.

Beyond communicating the KPI and influencing behavior, what is the purpose of the communication plan and how will it be used to achieve this purpose?

## Identifying Tools

Decide what tools will be used to accomplish the defined goals. These tools can be anything from a simple flyer to a glossy magazine to a meeting. Do not overlook less obvious tools such as posters, report covers and websites. Brainstorm ideas with your team.

## Establishing a Timetable

Once audiences, objectives, goals, and tools have been identified there may be a need to have certain things in place before you introduce this specific KPI. Or, you may want to meter out a series of KPIs in such a way as to allow people to adapt to the changes these will bring.

## Auditing the Results

Build into your plan a method for measuring results. Your evaluation might take the form of:

- A monthly report on work in progress;

- Formalized department reports for presentation at staff meetings;

- Periodic briefings for the manager and the department heads;

- A year-end summary for the annual report.

This is not simply auditing the KPI results: it must go further. For example, the leading KPI is there to influence and measure certain behaviors and habits. Has this been achieved or are we simply doing what we need to do to get the numbers our manager wants? If the behavior is not present, it is important to identify why and to develop a remedial plan.

## Defining a Transition Plan

I mentioned earlier that we must establish aggressive, but attainable, targets. When there are multiple steps to achieving your end goal, it is important to establish a transition plan whereby improvement and sustainability are defined at each stage.

## Defining an Action Plan

What happens if the target is not met? Presumably, something must be done to redress the situation. Unfortunately most organizations have only a cursory idea of what this action entails and even fewer have a concerted, agreed upon action plan in the event that the target is not met.

For every leading KPI, an action plan must be developed and approved by management before launching the KPI. Through this approval process the owner of the KPI is given authority to put the action plan in motion in the event that the target is not met.

If the organization is not prepared to define an action plan it may be that it does not truly believe in the benefit of this KPI and the value of putting measures in place to redress any shortfalls. If you are not prepared to take action then the KPI brings little value to the organization and should be eliminated.

## Limiting the Number of KPIs per Individual

It is not unusual for a person to track many KPIs. A simple guideline is to limit the number of KPIs per individual to five. Beyond this it will be difficult for the person to stay on top of the KPIs they are assigned and the results will be affected.

Most organizations therefore select a certain number of KPIs and simply ignore the rest. This is not the best solution. If the process element measured by the KPI is important to your organization it should be measured and reviewed. But we do not want to overwhelm the individual with too many KPIs, as they will lose focus. So what do we do?

To answer this let's borrow a page from quality control. In this field we control certain parameters through frequent measurements and audit others. The audit points are not unimportant but we either cannot measure these continuously or a longer measurement frequency suffices to meet our needs.

This same principle can be applied to KPIs. You should measure every KPI but decide if the particular measurement is a control point or an audit point. For example if there are 20 KPIs that I should be following and we apply the 5 maximum rule; I should therefore select 5 control point KPIs and relegate the other 15 KPIs to audit points. If over a period of time one of my control KPIs is always performing brilliantly but one of my audit KPIs is not, nothing precludes my changing the status of each so that the good control KPI becomes an audit KPI and the bad actor audit KPI becomes a control KPI.

# KPI Parameter Definition Template

Here is an example of a form you may wish to use to define your KPIs.

| Information ||
|---|---|
| Metric | |
| Definition | |
| Formula | |
| Owner | |
| Initial Target | |
| World Class Target | |
| Measuring Method | |
| Type of Metric | |
| Measuring Frequency | |
| Reference Source | |
| Control/Audit Point | |
| Parent KPI | |
| Child KPI(s) | |
| **Communication / Deployment Plan** ||
| Desired Behavior Targeted by KPI | |
| Impact of not Achieving the Objective | |
| Target Audience (Site Specific) | |
| Who Impacts the Metric | |
| Communicate Tools | |
| Meeting Where KPI is Reported | |
| Timeline for Introduction | |
| Auditing Method | |
| Changes Needed to Introduce the KPI | |
| Things to Communicate Prior to Introduction | |
| **Transition Plan** ||
| | |
| **Action Plan** (If we miss the target) ||
| | |

# KPI Hierarchy

As discussed in the introduction, leading KPIs measure the process that ensures the results, while the results are measured using lagging KPIs. Senior management and shareholders are predominantly interested in the results, but we cannot manage the results, we can only manage the process that leads to the results. A successful organization should report its organizational performance to senior management, and shareholders using lagging KPIs – while measuring and managing the process that produces the performance – through the use of leading KPIs.

A quantifiable correlation between the KPIs managing the process to those reporting the performance is essential because it defines the value each element of the process brings to the organization. This helps management decide on which activity, improvement initiative or capital project to invest the organization's resources and efforts. The correlation also helps identify KPIs that are meaningful to specific individuals and groups at each level of the organization. These KPIs measure and communicate the elements that the person or group can influence.

To quantify each element's contribution we must first map out the parent-child relationship between KPIs, starting with the organizational goals. We call this the KPI Hierarchy. These relationships are not always easy to quantify and we often need to make estimates or determine ratios. Nonetheless, this exercise is an important one since it unifies vision and direction between the organizational levels, provides a measure of the person's contribution and empowers people at every level to work towards the organization's success.

It is not unusual for organizations to not be ready to quantify the interrelationship, both in terms of the knowledge needed to do so and in terms of the group's readiness to accept the rankings. In such a case, it may be best to leave the ranking for a future date and focus on applying the defined KPIs.

The following are examples of a KPI hierarchy. This should be developed in collaboration with the stakeholders.

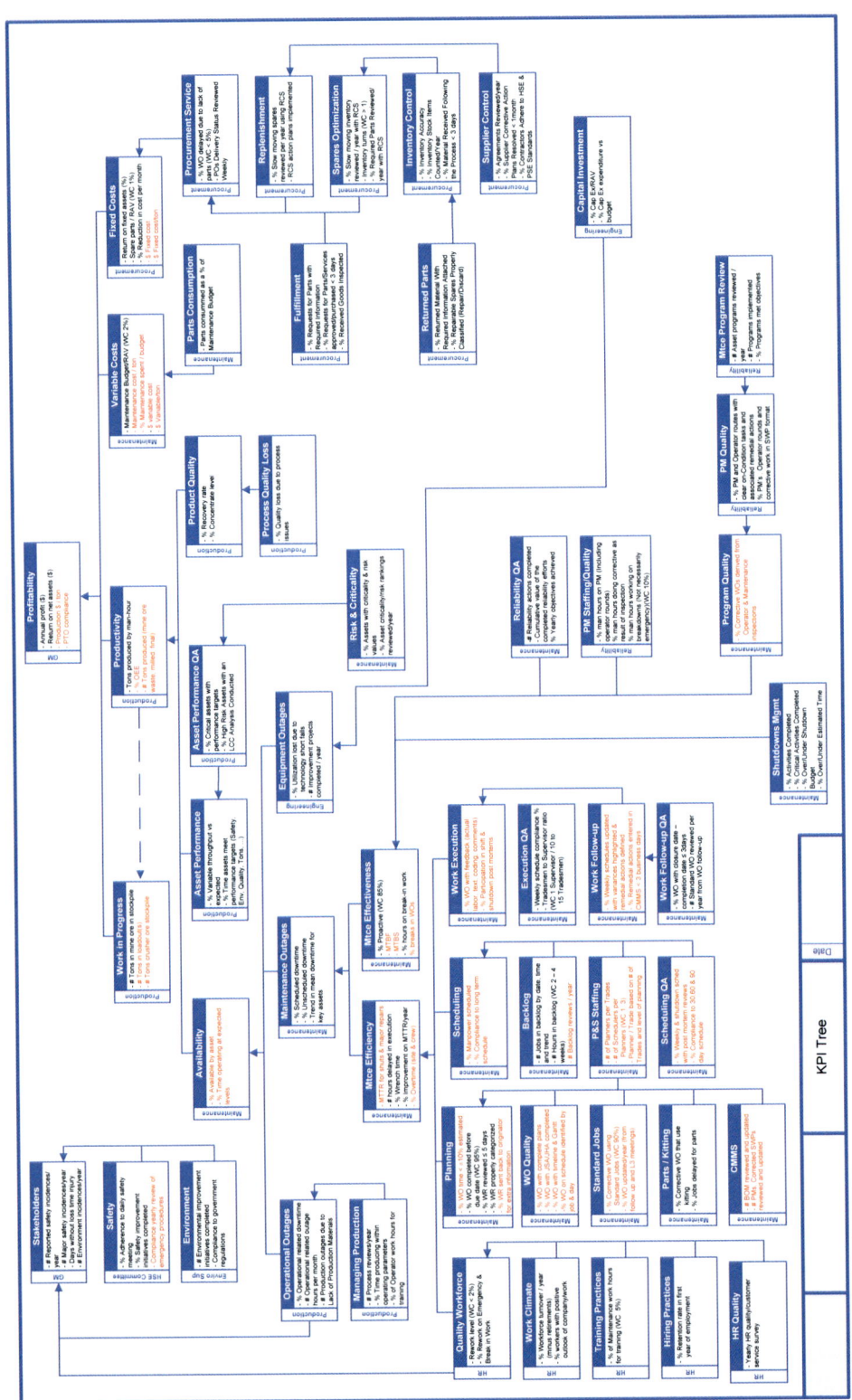

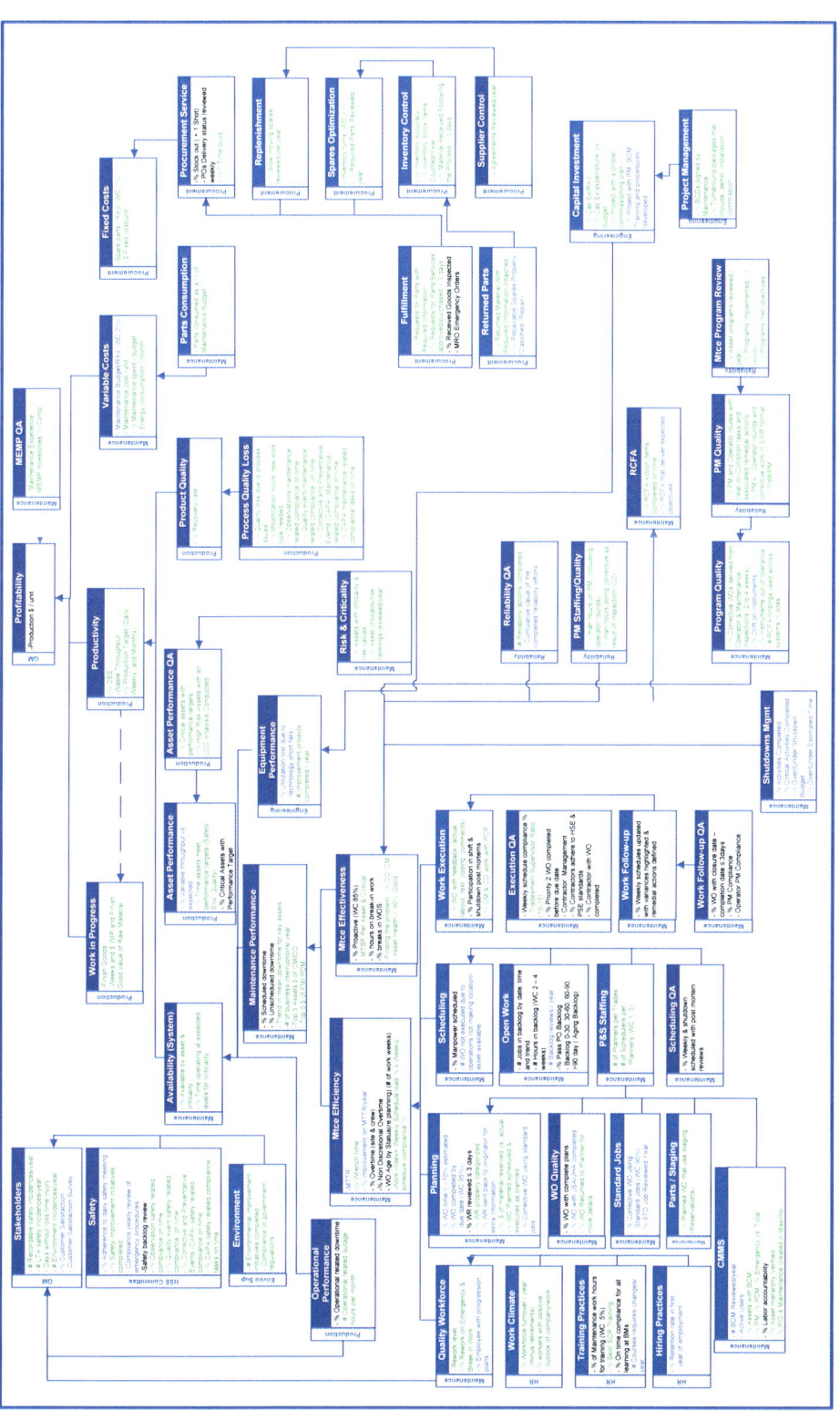

Effective Key Performance Indicators

## Weighting Factors

There is often significant interaction between the various leading KPIs. For example, a promotional campaign's effectiveness will be affected by the advantages (or lack of advantages) its products have over the competition. These advantages are represented by product development KPIs.

Though the interaction between the various leading KPIs makes it difficult to quantify their respective impact on the parent KPI, it is important to do so because it will help the organization make strategic decisions with respect to resources, efforts and investments. One way to define these relationships is to use weighting factors.

It is usually difficult to precisely quantify the weighting factors, and a certain amount of estimation is required. Interestingly, people in the organization, though often nervous about doing so, are usually the best at making these estimates. If they are truly engaged and passionate about the merits of this element, they will have a reasonable understanding of its impact on the parent KPI.

# Physical Asset Management KPI Examples

Following are a few KPI examples. This partial list is meant as a guide but by no means should it be used as your list. I recommend that you convene a multi-disciplinary team to develop a list of KPIs that is specific to your organizational needs. This same team will also complete the detailed description for each leading KPI. The following KPIs have been grouped in business elements for your convenience.

## Business focus KPIs

- % Assets with criticality and risk values
- % Asset criticality/risk rankings reviewed/year
- % Critical assets with performance targets
- # Improvement projects completed/year

# Performance Assurance KPIs
(usually set at the asset level and site level)

- # Reported safety incidences/year
- # Major safety incidences/year
- # Days since loss time incident
- # Reportable environmental spills/year
- # Days since last reportable environmental spill
- Tons/day, week, month, year
- % Recovery rate
- Cost/ton
- % Maintenance/Operational budget
- % Maintenance/RAV
- % Spare parts/RAV
- % Retention rate for new employees

# Work Identification KPIs

- % Proactive
- % WR/WO validated
- # Assets reviewed with a formal work identification methodology in a year.
- % Assets reviewed with a formal work identification methodology in a year.
- % Available man-hours used for modifications.
- % Corrective work derived from PdMs
- CBM execution index: Count and age of outstanding corrective work identified through condition monitoring.

- MTBF/MTBD: Trend in Mean Time Between Failures or Mean Time Between Downs for key identified asset types.

- % Break-in: The percentage of actual hours charged to break-in work (urgent and emergency).

- Reliability execution index: The percentage of reliability actions completed on time.

- Reliability $ value added: The cumulative value of the completed reliability efforts.

## Planning KPIs

- % Planned

- % Work Orders with all of the labor assignment, task duration, work priority, early start, late finish and work group fields completed. (World Class: 95 percent)

- % Work Orders with man-hour estimates within 10% of actual over the last month. (World Class: 90 percent)

- % Work Orders with parts list identical to planned over the last month. (World Class: 90 percent)

- MDT: The trend in Mean Down Time for key identified asset types.

## Scheduling KPIs

- % Actual scheduled available man-hours to total available man-hours over the last month. (World Class: 85 percent)

- % Work Orders that have a Scheduled Date earlier or equal to the late finish date. (World Class: 95 percent)

- # Jobs in the backlog.

- Number of planned hours in the backlog.
  (World Class: 2 to 4 weeks)

- Work index: Weekly schedule load percentage multiplied by that week's schedule compliance percentage.

## Execution KPIs

- % Wrench time. (World Class: 60 percent)

- % Completed work orders that include the following information: Actual labor hours worked, asset downtime, work order status (complete or incomplete) and materials. (World Class: 95 percent)

- % Work orders requiring rework due to improper execution. (World Class: < 2 percent)

- % Manpower dedicated to training. (World Class: 5 percent)

- % Manpower dedicated to modifications.
  (World Class: 4 – 5 percent)

## Follow up KPIs

- % Work orders with closure date minus completion date ≤ 3 days. (World Class: > 95 percent)

- # Standard work order reviews per year generated from the follow-up element.

- # Corrective work orders generated from the follow-up element.

# Deployment

## Deployment versus Implementation

Typical stages of an improvement initiative include develop and implement. Unfortunately the vast majority of improvement initiatives fail or are not sustainable. One of the reasons for this is that we tend to focus on either the technical or the cultural elements of the initiative but rarely both with sufficient emphasis to make the whole successful. Implementation by its definition tends to have a technical penchant. Therefore I like to separate implementation into two phases: implement and deploy, where implement incorporates the technical elements while deploy deals with the cultural elements. Up to this point this book has dealt with the development and implementation of an effective asset management organization. This section deals with its deployment.

Deployment is a crucial phase to developing an effective asset management organization and includes the development and application of a communication plan, control plan and, at times, a transition plan.

# Communication Plan

Creating awareness is an important first step toward building target-audience understanding, influencing opinion and motivating behavior. But there is much more required to execute a successful awareness campaign.

Over-communication is a lifestyle. Information bombards the senses from every conceivable source, every waking moment of the day. Communication channels have expanded. Not only are there more choices within mediums, but also more mediums from which to choose.

To create awareness, I suggest a communication plan. We spoke about a communication plan with respect to the individual KPIs. When applying an effective organizational engineering program, you should develop a communication plan that meets the needs of each individual item on a tactical level. You should also consider the strategic requirements of the plan and of the process.

A communication campaign includes not only ongoing communication, but also a program launch and an annual review of the plan. Typically, I like to use a rolling 3-year plan that is aligned with the corporate requirements.

## Committees and Teams

To properly manage the initiative and ensure results it is important to have well-established committees and groups and provide information to the site personnel on a regular basis. These generally include the following:

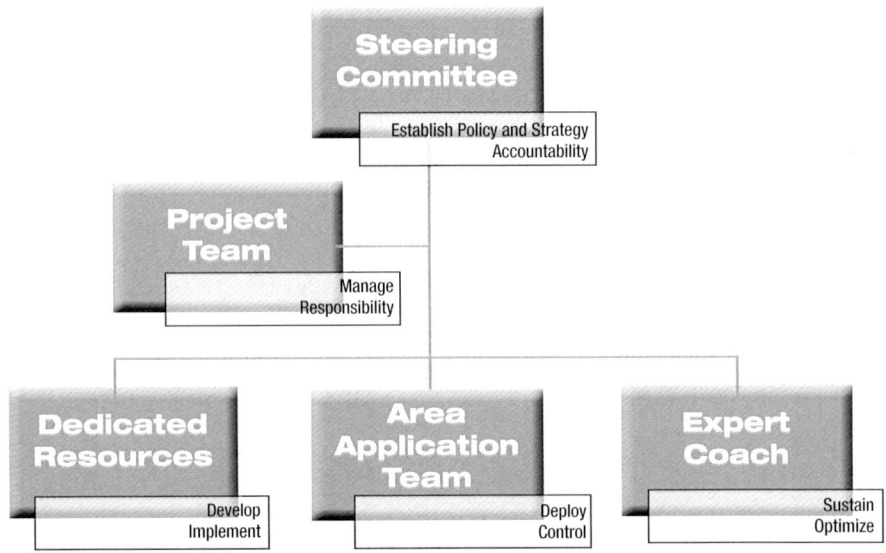

The Steering Committee plays a different role than the Project Team and is usually made up of senior staff members. Their role is to establish the initiative's policies and strategies. The Project Team is responsible to manage the initiative so as to meet the set policies and strategies. An important distinction here is that the Project Team constantly monitors the initiative's progress and adherence to the established direction while the Steering Committee periodically reviews the direction it has set to determine if this is still the right course to take.

On the bottom I listed three roles or groups: The Dedicated Team, the Area Application Team and the Expert Coach. Before discussing these roles we must first look at how to manage the deployment effort. Deployment involves people and culture change. It is usually very difficult, if not impossible, to affect this change across a whole site in one shot. Therefore I like to apply the new organizational processes one area at a time and only move to the next area once we've achieved a certain level of success. This is a depth versus breadth approach.

The Area Application Team is made up of the people in the area who own the process and who need to change how they do things. Developing and implementing the change takes effort and time, something that we usually have little of. Therefore we need Dedicated Resources to provide the manpower necessary to do this. As the Dedicated Team completes its work it moves to the next area while the Area Team continues to deploy the new processes and practices. Typically the practices and processes developed by the sustaining team will need some adjustment and lessons learned will provide opportunities to optimize. This is the role of the Expert Coach. Without the presence of the Coach, the Dedicated Team would be called back to support the area, hampering their ability to develop and implement for the next area.

## Creating Awareness in Continuum

Throughout the project and afterwards it is important to ensure awareness of the project and its progress at all levels of the organization.

Before starting the project a Project Charter is developed and presented to the site's management team to validate and ensure commitment to the process and objectives. The project will require a significant amount of effort from a number of individuals and it is important that this be quantified and agreed to before starting.

A progress report should be posted at a number of strategic places within the site and regularly updated as to progress, milestone achievements and problems. A selection of success metrics should also be posted and all success metrics should be reviewed during the committee meetings.

The managers should host regular town hall meetings with their staff to keep them informed of the project's progress as well as to identify concerns and suggestions. The project manager should generate weekly progress reports with success metrics, completed activities and next week's activities. Issues and action plans to resolve these should be included.

# Transition Plan/ Maturity Plan

Though there may be ultimate targets, the current levels may be so far removed from them that it is difficult to envision how these goals can be achieved. If the target seems unattainable to those tasked to meet it they may give up before even trying. In these cases, a roadmap is required to outline gradual increases in the target. The roadmap should include the stages, a timeline and activities to migrate from one stage to the next. Though gradual, each stage of the roadmap should be aggressive and attainable. This roadmap can become part of a maturity model.

A maturity model is a set of structured levels that describe how well the behaviors, practices and processes of an organization can reliably and sustainably produce the required outcome.

Sometimes organizations focus only on some aspects of the process improvement rather than a more holistic approach. This will lead to an imbalance in the improvement process and hamper or stop the projected gains. A gap analysis can provide guidance as to where to start but there comes a point that progress in all elements is essential.

# Control Plan

*"To manage you must be able to control and to control you must be able to measure"* - Peter Drucker

## Success Metric Groupings
The following are examples of possible project success metrics. I usually group these in three categories:

- **Accomplishments:** Milestones, stage gates and competency development.

- **Process:** Leading KPIs.

- **Financial:** Cost savings and production increases.

## Milestones

Milestones are identified directly on the project plan and are used as control metrics to measure project progress.

## Stage Gates

A stage gate process is a conceptual and operational roadmap for moving a project from start to finish. Stage gates divide the effort into distinct stages separated by management decision gates. The team must successfully complete a prescribed set of tasks and activities in each stage prior to obtaining management approval to proceed to the next stage.

## Competency Development

I like the "*Tell me, Show me, Coach me*" competency development process.

- Tell me is achieved through awareness sessions.

- Show me is achieved through formal training courses.

- Coach me is achieved through on-the-job coaching. As part of the coaching process, students are put through hands-on testing to ensure that they have reached the right level of competency.

## Contingency Planning

A very complex project with a significant human component will require that you make a number of assumptions. For the most part these will prove to be correct but there will undoubtedly be a few surprises. Also, as the organization progresses and matures through the project you will regularly revisit your priorities during the Steering Committee meetings. This will bring about some changes to the project activities and duration. I recommend that management develop a contingency plan to deal with possible unforeseen requirements.

# Conclusion

This book is meant to be a practical guide rather than a thesis on organizational engineering. As such it was kept short and to the point with specific examples on how to develop and deploy a physical asset management organization. You undoubtedly have some or even many of these elements already established within your organization and may only need a few additions. I nonetheless recommend that you take a moment to reflect on how successful you are in being system dependent, how well you manage your meetings and how effectively you use your KPIs.

No matter how advanced you are, if there is an opportunity to improve, I recommend the following steps: analyze your current state, define desired state, develop a simple plan, establish reasonable goals and identify the number and skill of resources needed to implement. In all cases you should solicit the help of a good coach and, when needed, resources to do the heavy lifting.

Hopefully this book has helped you discover the benefits of developing and deploying a world-class physical asset management organization and helped instill a sense of urgency to do so. To quote a good friend: "It's never too early to start but it is sometimes too late." In other words don't wait too long.

Enjoy the journey!

# Bio

### J.R. Paul Lanthier P. Eng.

Facilitator, practitioner, trainer, coach, mentor, project manager, practice lead, and director. Paul has worked in the fields of asset management, reliability and maintenance at all levels in several industry sectors around the world.

A recognized technical leader, Paul is a regular guest speaker at conferences, conducts webinars and has written a number of papers.

Asset Management and Reliability are technical, tactical and strategic exercises that consider human and organizational requirements in order to ensure sustainability. As a practicing leader, Paul champions efforts in this field to ensure that the approaches are holistic, sustainable and practical. These must consider both the technical and human aspects of change.

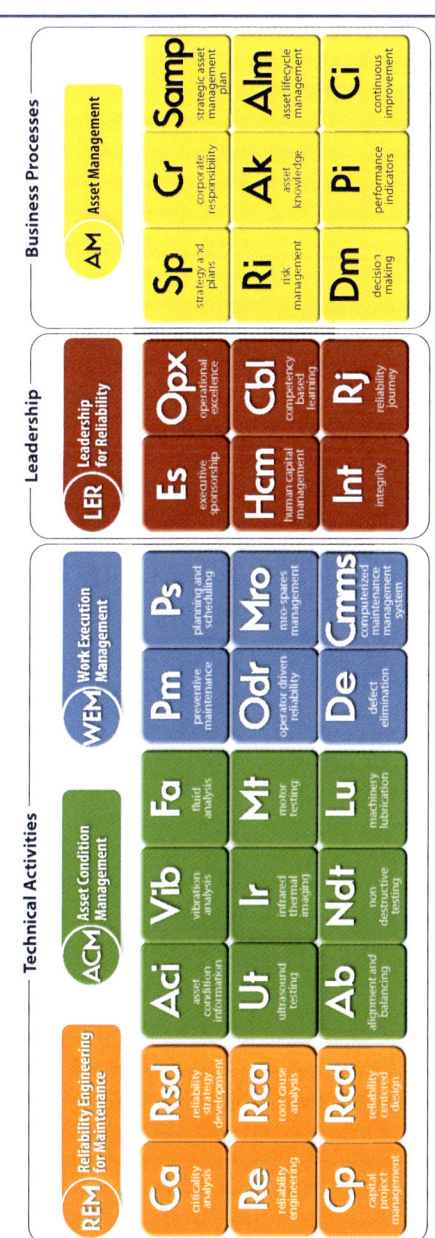

# ABOUT RELIABILITYWEB.COM

Created in 1999, Reliabilityweb.com provides educational information and peer-to-peer networking opportunities that enable safe and effective reliability and asset management for organizations around the world.

## ACTIVITIES INCLUDE:

**Reliabilityweb.com®** (www.reliabilityweb.com) includes educational articles, tips, video presentations, an industry event calendar and industry news. Updates are available through free email subscriptions and RSS feeds. **Confiabilidad.net** is a mirror site that is available in Spanish at www.confiabilidad.net.

**Uptime® Magazine** (www.uptimemagazine.com) was launched in 2005 that is highly prized by the reliability and asset management community.

**Reliability Leadership Institute® Conferences and Training Events** (www.reliabilityleadership.com) offer events that range from unique, focused-training courses and seminars to small focused conferences to large industry-wide events, including the International Maintenance Conference (IMC), MaximoWorld and The RELIABILITY 4.0 Digital Transformation Conference™ (TRC) East and West.

**MRO-Zone Bookstore** (www.mro-zone.com) is an online bookstore offering a reliability and asset management focused library of books, DVDs and CDs published by Reliabilityweb.com.

**Association of Asset Management Professionals** (www.maintenance.org) is a member organization and online community that encourages professional development and certification and supports information exchange and learning with 50,000+ members worldwide.

### A Word About Social Good

Reliabilityweb.com is mission-driven to deliver value and social good to the reliability and asset management communities. *Doing good work and making profit is not inconsistent*, and as a result of Reliabilityweb.com's mission-driven focus, financial stability and success has been the outcome. For over a decade, Reliabilityweb.com's positive contributions and commitment to the reliability and asset management communities have been unmatched.

### Other Causes

Reliabilityweb.com has financially contributed to include industry associations, such as SMRP, AFE, STLE, ASME and ASTM, and community charities, including the Salvation Army, American Red Cross, Wounded Warrior Project, Paralyzed Veterans of America and the Autism Society of America. In addition, we are proud supporters of our U.S. Troops and first responders who protect our freedoms and way of life. That is only possible by being a for-profit company that pays taxes.

I hope you will get involved with and explore the many resources that are available to you through the Reliabilityweb.com network.

Warmest regards,
Terrence O'Hanlon
CEO, Reliabilityweb.com

---

Reliabilityweb.com®, Uptime®, The RELIABILITY Conference™, MaximoWorld and Reliability Leadership Institute® are the trademarks or registered trademarks of Reliabilityweb.com and its affiliates in the USA and in several other countries.